**NON-FICTION**

A Soldier's Tale

Library Learning Information

Idea Store® Canary Wharf
Churchill Place
Canary Wharf
London E14 5RB

020 7364 4332
www.ideastore.co.uk

Created and managed by
Tower Hamlets Council

Published in 2004 by:
Nelson Thornes Ltd
Delta Place
27 Bath Road
CHELTENHAM
GL53 7TH
United Kingdom

04 05 06 07 08 / 10 9 8 7 6 5 4 3 2 1

A catalogue record for this book is available from the British Library

ISBN 0 7487 9004 7

Cover illustration by Zhenya Matysiak
Page make-up by Tech-Set, Gateshead

Printed in Croatia by Zrinski

Introduction

The Second World War lasted from 1939 to 1945. Lawrence Oakes (known as Richard to his friends) was called up to fight. Like millions of others, he had no say in the matter.

This is his story.

1

1939

The envelope landed in the hall. I took out my call-up papers. I was going to war. I was going to fight Hitler with the rest of them.

I didn't want to fight. I'd just got married for a start. I'd never held a gun in my life. I was happy driving my van around the shops. Now all that was over. I was going to be a soldier.

I had to go see the doctors at the Town Hall. There were a lot of men there. They'd all had their call-up papers like me. I don't think any of them were very pleased.

I went back home and told my wife Bessie I'd been passed A1. That meant I was in good shape. It meant there were no excuses.

I had to go to Portsmouth. I kissed Bessie goodbye at the station. She was in tears. We didn't know when we'd see each other again.

The steam train chugged out of the station. I got into a crowded carriage. There were soldiers everywhere.

4

I'd never felt so alone. I'd never been so far away in my life. To me, Portsmouth was the other end of the world.

It was nearly midnight when the train pulled into Portsmouth. There were Red-Caps everywhere. Their job was to keep an eye open for anyone going AWOL.

The army camp was near the sea. I followed some others and saw lights winking over the water. A sergeant was up ahead, giving orders. He asked me my name. I told him. He pointed to one of the huts behind.

'That's your new home. Aren't you a lucky man? You'd better get up there sharp before somebody gets your bed.'

I was dog tired and my case felt like a lump of lead. I was in the army now. I wished I wasn't. But there was nothing I could do about it.

2

There were 50 of us to a hut. We had a locker for our things. I soon learnt to put everything in order. If your bed wasn't neat the sergeant tipped it up. Army rules had to be obeyed at all times.

Two days later I got kitted out. Two shirts, two vests, two long pants, battledress, sidehat, socks, boots, PT kit, two blankets, a jersey and coat. The uniform was like sandpaper against your skin.

A lot of the men weren't fit. I was lucky. I'd done some running at home. We had to do a 10-mile run in full battledress. Anyone who slacked had to peel potatoes or clean the lavs. We had to have a cold shower when we got back. Even the men who hadn't been fit got used to it in the end. If we were to be any use as soldiers, we had to be fit.

The CO found out I'd driven a van. He gave me a job training men to drive an army truck. We did target practice using Lee Enfield rifles and the bigger Lewis guns.

We took spells on guard duty, two hours on, two hours off. We were told to keep our eyes open. One of the men tried to arrest the CO. The CO let him off for being keen.

I had a 24 hour pass every three weeks. But it wasn't long enough to get back home to Bessie. It was no use spending your free time anywhere but in Portsmouth. In any case, I'd soon be leaving Portsmouth for good.

3

South Africa

Without warning we were put on a train for London.
I spent a few weeks learning how to fire a big gun
called a howitzer. We had to keep practising until
each man knew what to do without thinking.

One day we were told to go to the store and get
tropical kit. You only wore that if you were going
somewhere hot. The next day we were put on a
Liverpool train. Liverpool was where the big ships
docked.

We found out we were going to South Africa. I'd
never been on a ship before. And this was the
biggest ship I'd ever seen. It was so full we had to
sleep on deck.

Soon we were at sea. Every day we had to keep fit.
Every day we had to do our rifle drill. No one was
allowed to smoke on deck in case German ships saw
the lit cigarette.

The weather got warmer. Flying fish skimmed
through the air. Dolphins swam along with us. I was
given a job taking food from the galley to the officers'

mess. In the galley fish were hanging from hooks. The fish were covered in cockroaches.

The cook said cockroaches meant good luck. It meant the ship wouldn't sink. 'Anyway,' he added, 'you'll be having that fish for your dinner tomorrow.'

I told him, 'You can eat it. I won't'. And I didn't.

Six weeks later we saw the lights of Cape Town. We were told we'd be in South Africa for ten days while we waited for another ship. Where would this other ship take us? No one knew. In the army, the officers told you nothing.

I spent the time sightseeing. It was good to be on dry land again. The war seemed a long way away.

4

India

A few months before I'd been a van driver. I was just a working man, no different from 1,000s of others. Now I'd been thrown into another world. Since I left the train at Portsmouth I'd crammed ten lives into one. And now I was sailing with the British Army to India. Why? I hadn't a clue.

We got to Bombay (now Mumbai) on the 16 September 1940. I'll never forget my first sight of the city. The stink of curry and drains. Beggars in rags. I was told there were rich people too, but I didn't see any.

We were marched along the docks. The sun beat down. There were flies everywhere. I was dreaming of an ice-cold beer. Currys were handed out instead. The men wouldn't eat them. It was too hot for curry.

After a rest, the CO marched us to the station. We were going to the town of Poona, about 200km away. We passed children begging. There were cows and ox-drawn carts. Thin hands were held out to us as we marched. 'Buckshee, sahib. Buckshee, sahib.' Spare a coin. It went on like that all the way to the station.

The carriages stank. The heat made me feel sick. In some of the carriages windows had been taken out for air. On the carriage roofs sat the locals. Some had a goat or a hen with them. It was a world I never knew existed.

The train got to Poona. We had a 2km march to Kirkee barracks. It was to be my home for the next ten months.

I soon found out more about India. When the rain came it turned Kirkee into a mud bath. It was followed by hot sun, which burnt the mud hard and made cracks in the ground. At night a million insects hummed.

There was no fighting here. We played football and kept up our gun practice.

We had to carry our dinner from the cook house to the canteen. If you weren't careful the food would be whipped off your plate by big birds called Black Kites. Chameleons ran across the walls and spiders hid under the lav seats. The odd snake also made its home in our lockers.

I went to the local market. People were cooking chickens by open drains. People were dirt poor. There were children everywhere. Some washed clothes in a stream. If I didn't want to walk back I took a nightmare ride in a gharrie.

Bit by bit I got used to it. But I never knew what we were there for. For us the war still didn't exist.

5

At Kirkee we learnt about map reading and how to use a compass. We had to find our way to a place the CO had given us on the map.

At one time we were told to follow a sheet tied to a gun. Our truck broke down. When I started it up again, I picked out what I thought was the sheet in the distance. It turned out to be an ox-cart. Hours later I caught up with the rest of the lads.

Once the army made up its mind what you were best at, they never forgot. I was back to training new drivers. I also had to test and mend new trucks.

They sent me on a mechanics course at Rawalpindi 2,000km to the north. This time the train had beds and showers.

I learnt a lot in a short time. The course should have lasted six weeks. But we were called back to Kirkee after ten days.

In my last night at Rawalpindi a Holy Man came to my tent. I was writing a letter to Bessie at the time. He wrote the words 'Mary Elizabeth' with a stick in the dust. It was my wife's full name.

'You've been through my things,' I told him.

'No, sahib.'

'Then how do you know my wife's name?'

'I know many things. Sahib, you will have a bad time. You will be wounded. But do not worry. You will go back home.' The man scraped the ground again. 'You will also have two sons. This is the name of your first son.'

He'd written 'Michael' in the dust.

After the war ended, we did have two sons. We called the first Michael. And I was wounded too. In fact, I was lucky to survive.

6

Iraq

We left India in August 1941. I'd been a soldier for nearly two years. And I'd never seen a German...yet.

Now we were sailing over the Indian Ocean. We were all in a good mood. We didn't know if there was danger ahead. We were young and full of life.

We landed at Basra, in Iraq. Our convoy was told to move to Shiber. All we saw for miles were sand hills, plus the odd camel or donkey.

We camped in tents. The first night we were there, a sandstorm whipped clouds of sand in the air. It found its way through every pinhole and stung our faces.

The sandstorm went as quickly as it had come. The desert was silent once more. Everything we had, even our pants, were full of sand. The place was alive with scorpions and spiders the size of a table tennis ball. Vultures flapped through the air. We sometimes took shots at them for practice.

One day we had news the Arabs had blown up the train which brought supplies to the camp. The

Colonel thought the supplies might be in a village up the track.

'I want you to find the stuff and get it back to base,' he told us. 'Don't shoot unless you have to. Fingers on the trigger, but don't press unless you're in real trouble.'

It was our first job. Forty of us drove off. At dawn we came to the Arab tents. An order was given to search for the supplies.

I went with a mate into the nearest tent. A man was pretending to be asleep. We got him up. Under his bed were boxes of tea, sugar, and coffee. The other lads found more supplies in the other tents. Just after sun-up we'd got it all back. Without a shot fired.

The rest of my time in Iraq I spent testing trucks in the sand. You had to know where you were. If you got lost in the desert you could be dead in a day. A mate of mine got lost. He survived by drinking water from the engine.

After a month we went in convoy to Baghdad. There were a thousand men with guns, vans, trucks and gun carriages. Then we moved on. Nobody knew where we were going. But we knew the war was not far away. We felt a jolt of excitement. We were sure it wouldn't be long before we met the Germans. In a way we wanted to meet them, to know the worst. We seemed to have been on the move forever.

We followed the River Euphrates. There were flocks of sheep. Goats and deer roamed the hills. There wasn't much food. Sometimes the Arabs would sell us some milk or an orange. Water was always a problem. We carried barely enough for our needs.

Our convoy speeded up. Now we were in Syria. We called ourselves 'The Flying Column' because we were moving fast now.

But not fast enough.

7

I don't know who saw it first. A German bomber,
flying low. We ran for the river and dived in the
reeds. The raid only lasted for a few minutes. It was
our first taste of war.

The next day we were on our way to Damascus. We
had a day's rest then set off West again. We got to
the next country, Jordan. Up mountain passes with
stones all over the road. One truck went over the top
and killed the driver.

Suddenly we were in low land. Below a hot sky we
saw the sea shining. It seemed as if it had been
painted blue, after our months in the desert.

We heard one of the officers mention Rommel. He was
one of the best men the Germans had. He was fighting
the British in the desert. A sense of excitement hung in
the air. We all knew now where we were going. We
were going to fight the German army in North Africa.

We went over the Suez Canal and into Egypt. It was
so hot your body ran with sweat. We slept under the
stars, in trucks and under them. Up at first light and
on our way west again. Big guns joined our column.
We never stopped. We were allowed no rest.

We pushed on through Libya. Vast plains of yellow sand. The blue Mediterranean below us. The guns and trucks threw up a fine dust. The air was like an oven.

Three days later I heard the far off boom of exploding shells. We were only a few kilometres away from the fighting. A ripple ran through my tummy. This was it. I was in it now. We all were. I felt in my pocket for my wife's photo. I wondered if I'd ever see her again.

8

Tobruk

I'd never stopped training since I was called up. Guns. Trucks. Manoeuvres. The army had made me fit. I had to stay fit to keep alive.

Fingers of smoke rose from the desert where the shells hit. British and German guns were firing at each other across the waste. Behind the lines were field hospitals and rows of trucks.

The din of exploding shells made you reel. Men lay dying or dead in the sand. You didn't just feel the danger. You smelt it.

I was in charge of a gun team. We were up before dawn. We dug a trench for the gun to be lowered into. We filled bags with sand to make a wall in case we took a hit. Nets were thrown over the guns to hide them. We had to dig a slit trench so we'd have somewhere to dive out of danger.

The big guns spat ribbons of fire across the sand. Sometimes the battle went on at night, and the desert was lit up like day. The officer in charge of our guns was killed. Another took his place. You were so afraid your guts turned to water.

The Germans had locked onto our guns. They opened fire at dawn. They picked off the British guns one by one in a line. A booted leg flew into the air. A chunk of metal took off the sergeant's arm. He dropped like a rag doll. A head rolled across the sand.

The German guns were now out of range. The British couldn't reach them. The gun next to me exploded. Next it would be us.

'Into the slit trench. Move!'

We dived into the trench. I hoped I'd die quickly. I didn't want to lie there screaming in pain.

Our gun burst into atoms above our heads. We had to draw back or we'd be dead. I saw the trucks some way back, and ran for them.

When I got there I saw they were full of holes.

9

I passed ten trucks before I found one that had no holes in it. I started the engine. The others came up and got in the back. But I could hardly turn the wheel. A splinter of metal stuck out of the tyre. I had a flat.

I could drive no more than 15mph. One of the men sat with me. We both took hold of the wheel. Then my mate took a bullet through the neck and slumped forward.

I grew weaker and weaker. I could hardly see what I was doing. Then we went over a sand ridge. The truck dug in the sand at the bottom and stopped.

I got down. As I did so a German tank came over the ridge. The captain got out. He held a handgun. The rest had rifles.

'Can you walk?' he asked in English.

'Not well.' I hadn't noticed in the truck. I'd been shot in the arm. And my leg was giving me pain.

'You are prisoners of war,' said the captain. 'I will take you to the First Aid post.'

I was put on the back of the tank. We were all taken behind the German lines. There was an ambulance in the sand. Inside a doctor was operating on injured soldiers. There was a man helping. His job was to bury the cut off arms and legs in the sand. The doctor dressed my arm and looked at my leg. He prodded the wound.

'Does that hurt?'

'No.'

'You go to hospital. They fix you up good.'

That night I lay on a stretcher looking at the stars. I shared a cigarette with an injured German. A German officer came up.

'You take it easy. You will go to Germany. You will be okay. Prisoner of war.' He walked off.

The German on the next stretcher smiled. 'Rommel' he said.

Rommel had spoken to me! I wondered what Bessie would say.

10

July 1942
Italy

In the morning we were taken up to a field hospital on the coast. They put my arm in a sling. My leg began to give me trouble.

We soon had to leave. More injured soldiers were arriving all the time. We were put on a hospital ship. By afternoon the desert had faded from view.

The doctor called my name. He took off my sling and looked at my arm.

'You have broken it. When we get on land, they make it good again.'

I rolled up my shorts. My leg was starting to swell. 'Could you take a look at my leg, doctor?'

'You lie on the table. Nurse, hold his waist.'

The doctor poked his knife in the wound. He took out some tweezers and put them in the hole. I felt nothing. Suddenly he gave a pull. He dropped something into a bowl.

'It is a bullet. It has hit the bone and bent. You want it?'

I put it in my pocket.

The ship docked at Naples. A train was waiting. We got on. Some could walk. Others were on stretchers. When all our names had been checked, the train started.

The carriages were crowded with wounded soldiers and POWs. After hours we reached Lucca. We were put on trucks. The trucks took us to a big hospital.

It was very clean. Nuns looked after us, and helped the doctors. I slept a lot of the time. Sometimes I helped the other men write letters home. For the first time we had enough to eat. There were Red Cross parcels every day. My leg got better. So did my arm. Ten months later I was fit again.

One morning some guards came into our ward. My name was called. We had to get ready. We were being taken to a POW camp.

We were marched to the station and put on a train. As darkness fell, we stopped at a small station. On a board it said Fara Sabina.

I wondered what lay in store.

11

POW Camp PG54

Our camp was in the Monti Sabini hills. There were fields as far as the eye could see. Around the camp was a wire fence. There were watchtowers with searchlights. Anyone trying to escape would be shot.

There were 3,000 POWS in the camp. We lived in tents, 60 to a tent. We slept on straw beds. We had watery stews made of turnips or cabbages. There was no meat. Some of the men went down with dysentery.

We were allowed a roll of bread every day. Cheese was given out once a month. The men used to fight for it. Hardly any Red Cross parcels came through in the first months.

Some of the men grew so hungry they took turnip tops out of the drains. They washed them and ate them raw. The water was bad. The taps were cut off at noon each day.

Our health went from bad to worse. The lavatories were trenches. Flies came around in swarms. Many men had lice in their hair. Washing and shaving was a thing of the past.

New POWS came in every day. One made a bucket from biscuit tins. Another made a clock. Their only tools were hands and stones. Yet even a stove was made.

Those who could joined in games for an hour a day. Those who couldn't told their story to a group.

Slowly, things began to get better. Wooden huts were built and the tents taken down. The Italians put in a pump for clean water. Red Cross food began to arrive.

We grew stronger. We began to organise things better. We put on shows. The shows lasted two hours. Even the Italian guards watched them.

I'd written to Bessie. She knew I was a POW. I was out of the war and safe. She wasn't to know that I'd soon be on the run.

12

Summer 1943
Freed from POW Camp

I'd just finished PT when I heard a din in the sky.
A Spitfire was chasing a German fighter over the
hills. The guards leaned by the fence. The sun beat
down on the camp. It was nearly mid-day.

Suddenly the Italian CO came out. He was with a
British officer. The officer told us all to line up. 'I've
just been speaking with the Camp Commander,' he
said. 'He has just told me the Italians are no longer
fighting in the war. He has asked me to tell you that
you are now free men.'

A cheer rang out. The camp gates were thrown
open. 'The British Army will be in Rome by
tomorrow,' the CO said. 'Rome's only 50km away.
You'll be able to join them. Stick together. Stay in
the woods. The UK troops will pick you up.

A wave of POWS pushed through the gates. I went
to get my things. What if the British Army didn't
reach Rome tomorrow? What about food? Which
way did we run? We might meet Germans instead
of the British.

One of the men kicked the stores door down.
We helped ourselves to food parcels and cigarettes.
A faint rattle of gunfire sounded from the hills.

We split into groups. Each group went its own way.
I found myself with a couple of South Africans, an
English mate and an Irishman. The sound of gunfire
grew nearer. We didn't know where the Germans
were. They could be all around us.

We ran off down a hillside full of prickly bushes.
The Irishman fell down. He let out a yell of pain and
gripped his leg. Escape was not going to be easy.

Our stolen food kept us going for a few days. We
kept clear of villages and stuck to the forest. We had
no map. When the food ran out we'd have to steal it.
We'd seen no British soldiers. We were on our own.

The Irishman's leg began to swell. He began to lag
behind. He rolled up his shorts. A black dot poked
through the skin. My English friend looked at me.
'It's a leaf from the prickly bushes. We'll have to get
it out.'

I had a razor blade. We boiled some stream water
on a wood fire and dropped the blade in a can to
sterilise it. While the others held the Irishman down
I cut into his swollen leg.

A trickle of blood came out. I cut again. The end of the leaf broke through the cut. One of the men had a pair of tweezers. I took a grip on the leaf and yanked hard. It came right out. It was as big as a man's hand.

The Irishman let out a scream, then smiled when he saw the leaf. We tore a strip off his shirt and bound up the wound. We were on our way again.

We moved slowly through the trees by day. At night we kept in the shadow of the hills.

In the moonlight we came upon a sort of straw hut. It was used by farmers working away from home. We went in and looked at what we had left. It wasn't much.

We decided we might have a better chance if we split. I shook hands with the others. I watched them creep into the moonlight. Now there was just me and my mate from the camp.

13

Montelibretti

We'd run out of food. We had to have help. I told my
mate I was going to a village we'd seen from the
hills. If they handed me over to the Germans, bad
luck. He came with me.

We felt as if everyone was staring at us as we walked
down the empty streets. An upstairs window
opened. A woman waved us to come in.

We followed her into a small room. She pulled a
radio from under some sacks. I could faintly hear the
BBC. I looked up and smiled.

She began to speak in Italian. It took us a long time
to make out what she was saying. We were to go
back to her house on Monday night. There'd be
someone else to help us.

Next Monday we found a man in the room. He told
us the Germans had found a lot of POWs and sent
them to a camp in Germany. Now the Germans were
on the look out for any other POWs on the run. He
said the Germans could tell the British because of
their army walk.

We thanked him for the information. For some weeks we hid in the straw hut. We visited the woman at night to listen to the radio. She gave us a meal. The word got around that we were hiding in the hut. Those in the village who wanted the British to win the war left food there for us.

We were always looking out for Germans. My friend and I split in the day. If one was caught, the other would still be free. We met in the hut after dark.

One night he told me a friend of the woman with the radio had offered to take him in. I wished him good luck. But now I was on my own. I started to get a fever. I couldn't stop shaking. I felt so tired I could hardly stand.

I remembered voices. When I woke up the sun was streaming through the door. People were looking at me. Saying things I couldn't understand. A woman put a blanket over me. I drifted off to sleep again.

When I woke it was dark. There were two men outside. They were holding a horse. They helped me climb up. They led the horse across the fields. I was only half-awake.

'You safe,' said one of the men in a whisper. 'We take you to Montelibretti. You stay with us.'

14

The Merzettis

They got me down from the horse and took me to a farm near the town. There was a room above the stable. Through the window I saw the hills bathed in moonlight.

When I awoke the fever had gone. I went over to the window. The sun shone over yellow fields and olive groves. I tried the door. It was bolted. More than anything, I needed food.

The bolt was drawn. A man came into the room. He made a sign to follow him downstairs. His family were sitting around a table eating a kind of porridge.

The man pointed to each person and named them. Then he pointed to himself: Giuseppi, Giuseppi Merzetti. I told them my name. Richard: Richard Oakes. Riccardo, in Italian.

'You eat with us, Riccardo,' the man said in Italian. It didn't take me long to finish my bowl. Already I felt much better. The children began to clear the table. I got up to help, but the mother wouldn't let me. Guiseppi watched from the door. He was in his work clothes. I wanted to join him, but he made a sign to show there were Germans about.

I wasn't happy staying in my room. Time dragged. I wondered what would happen to the Merzettis if the Germans found out they'd taken me in. Would they have their house burned down? Shot? I didn't want to think about it.

The months went by. Guiseppi let me help in the olive groves when the German's weren't about. I grew fit and brown in the sun. But eating was a problem. The family made stews of dandelion and potato leaves. These strange foods made my guts ache.

One day I had an idea. Guiseppi gave his pig potatoes to eat. I thought I'd like some chips. I offered to carry the potatoes to the pig. On the way I stole six. I was going to make some chips.

Guiseppi's wife followed every move I made. Everyone came to watch. They'd never seen chips before. It wasn't long before they'd eaten the lot.

I was like one of the family. Three years before I'd been driving a van loaded with drinks. I'd married a wife I'd hardly seen. Now I was sharing a home with a family of Italians. They risked their lives looking after me.

Then I heard that a German officer had moved into a villa at the edge of the village. My days on the run might soon be over.

15

The summer went on. I was as brown as a nut. Every day I learnt more Italian words.

One day Guiseppi's son, Pietro, came home from school crying. He'd been put in a corner because he couldn't do his sums. I said I'd teach him. In three weeks he'd learnt his tables and his sums. Now he came top of the class. He said his teacher didn't know how it could have happened!

The family were all out one day. I had a glass of Giuseppi's wine in my hand. I was thinking of Bessie. She hadn't heard from me in months. She'd think I'd been killed.

Suddenly, footsteps sounded outside. I looked through the window. German soldiers were coming to the house. I rushed upstairs. As I reached my room the downstairs door crashed open.

Any minute they'd be coming upstairs. I opened the window and climbed out onto the roof. I hid for what seemed like hours. At last they went away.

That wasn't the only close call. Another time I went to visit my English friend who'd been helped by someone else in the town. We were playing cards upstairs when we heard a bang on the door. We both froze. We waited. There were no more bangs. We thought we were safe. Then we heard the door open.

I looked over the landing. A German was coming into the house. He was looking for escaped POWs.

We dived under my friend's bed. The first boot sounded on the stairs. At the same time we heard the family's dog barking. It followed the German soldier upstairs. We held our breath.

The soldier sat on the bed and lit a cigarette. The dog saw us and started to yap. I shut my eyes. Suddenly the dog padded downstairs. The German followed. We couldn't believe our luck.

How many lives did I have left? Today, tomorrow, the Germans would find me. What would happen to the Merzettis? Giving help to the enemy was a serious thing. I didn't want anything to happen to them. I had to leave their house. I had to get them out of danger.

Another brush with the Germans helped me make up my mind. I was looking after the fire for Mrs Merzetti when I saw a German standing by the open door. He was looking for POWs on the run. Now we were face to face.

He asked me where the woman of the house was. He asked in Italian. I knew he thought I was one of the family. I was burnt brown by the sun. I looked like any other Italian farm worker.

'Who are you?' he asked.

I knew enough Italian to tell a lie. 'I'm a cousin of the family. I'm from the next village. Come in. There's wine on the table.'

I kept his glass topped up. He showed me his scars where he'd been wounded. He was a good man. He was tired of the war. And so was I.

When he left, my heart was hammering. I don't know if he suspected me. I made up my mind to hide in the forest. Things were getting too hot for the Merzettis.

16

The Cave

I found a place to hide. Giuseppi gave me a spade. I could see his house 3km away. He said he'd hang a sheet from the window if it was safe to come to the house to eat.

I dug out a small cave. It took me three months. I had a slab for a fire and a shelf for food. I had a straw bag to sleep on. I spent nights in the cave. By day I was on the move.

Water was a problem. One day I saw a shepherd put a reed in the ground and drink. That night I did the same. I filled my old kettle with good water. I used a stream for washing in.

Mrs Merzetti worried about me. She made me take a hot bath when I came to the house for food. That made the cave feel colder when I went back.

One morning my guts were hurting. I must have eaten something bad. Maybe a walk in the cool forest would make me feel better.

I got to a rock in the trees and sat down. I felt ill. I must have drifted asleep. I awoke to a gun in my ribs. A man with a beard stood there. He wasn't a German. Who was he?

He made a sign for me to go with him. He kept his gun on me all the time. We got to a large cave. There were four other men with guns.

'Who are you?' he asked, in Italian.

'I'm English. I escaped from a POW camp.'

'Have you papers?'

I showed them a photo of my wife. And her last letter to me. The first man started to laugh. They all joined in. Wine was handed around.

'You English. You our friend. This forest full of bad men. Germans. Here. You have this. You shoot, eh?' He handed me a gun, and let me go.

I didn't know who they were. Italy was in chaos. There were all sorts of groups fighting for this or that. Every day the sound of tanks and bombs grew louder. The war was moving closer to my hiding place.

It was only a matter of time before I was caught. For months every nerve in my body had been tense.

Every sound I heard seemed loud. Every shadow might be a German. I couldn't go on like this much longer.

At 5 o'clock one morning, things were decided for me. I felt a jolt in my sleep. I blinked and opened my eyes. A German officer was looking down at me.

'Do you have a gun?' he asked, in English.

I shook my head. I was glad I'd hidden the gun I'd been given.

'I'm a POW,' I said.

'Do you have any proof?'

I showed him Bessie's photo. He gave it back to me.

He saw a jar of jam on the shelf. 'Where did you get this food?' he asked.

'From the town.'

'Which town?'

'I don't know.'

'Did you steal it?'

'No. I swapped a pair of boots for it.'

'And your clothes?'

'I found them in a barn.'

'You stole them?'

'Yes.'

They led me away. As I went, I saw the towel I'd used for my wash hanging out to dry. I'd given the game away.

They led me through Monelibretti at gunpoint. Crowds came to watch. I saw a face I knew. Pietro, who I'd helped with his sums.

He ran off. I knew what he'd tell Guiseppi. 'The soldiers have led Riccardo away.'

17

May 1944 – April 1945

Stalag V11A

The German CO looked up from his desk. 'You're going back to the camp,' he said.

I was taken back to the camp I'd escaped from a year before. But not for long. The war was all around us. We had to be moved.

We were marched 40km to a train station. There were a lot of us on the move. Some were ill. Some were wounded. Some didn't make it.

My feet were bleeding. After weeks in the cave, I wasn't well. A German soldier saw I was in trouble. He gave me a lift to the station in a truck.

There were a line of cattle trucks. There were 50 to a truck. Each truck had a tiny window with bars, and a bucket at one end for a lavatory. The doors were shut and we moved out of the station.

The train went slowly. Sometimes it stopped. The wagons began to stink.

For three days we didn't eat. Some of the men died.
One soldier knelt on the floor. He had a chisel. He
began to lift up a plank.

'When the train stops, I'm getting out,' he said. 'Does
anyone want to join me?'

The train was going at walking speed. He dropped
with two others through the hole in the floor.
Someone put back the planks. The train rumbled on.

We stopped again and again. Bread rolls were given
out by the Germans. Now the air was cooler. We
were in the mountains. We were being taken to
Germany.

We got to the end of our journey. Our new camp was
near Munich. It was called Stalag V11A. There were
60,000 POWs there. New POWs were arriving every
day. There were Russians, Americans, Canadians
and British.

The Germans were always on the look out for anyone
trying to escape. There were parades every day.
Heads were counted.

The Americans and British were bombing Munich.
Some of us had to leave the camp and help in the
city. I was shocked by what I saw.

The city had been almost wiped out. We helped dig German people from the rubble. My heart went out to them. Sometimes British POWs were killed along with the Germans they were helping.

I remember a little boy lifting up bricks and gazing into the hole. The bricks had once been his house. He was saying 'mother' and 'father' in German. His parents had been buried alive. I put my arm around him. Nothing would bring his parents back. That night I cried myself to sleep.

A few days later I had to help at Munich station. There were bomb holes everywhere. The gas mains had been blown up. Fires flared into the sky. Four thousand people had been in the station. Now it was just rubble. Trains had been blown across the platforms. Bodies lay everywhere.

I felt ill. I seemed to be floating in air. I could hardly walk. I had a picture in my head of someone in white. It turned out to be a camp doctor. I came to six weeks later. I'd had meningitis. He'd given me penicillin. The Red Cross had sent it from England. It had saved my life.

The war was coming to a close. The camp was on the edge of a riot. Germany was in chaos. If I survived, I'd soon be free.

18

Going Home

Now I heard the drone of British and American planes every day. Shells landed near the camp. I wondered if I'd ever see Bessie again.

Then suddenly, the planes stopped. The war had ended.

I felt numb. I was put on a plane and taken back to England. I looked down through the clouds and saw the green fields below. I couldn't believe I was still alive. I couldn't believe I'd survived.

When I got down, I sent a telegram to my wife. It said simply: 'Home today. With love. Richard.'

That afternoon I found myself walking up the street I'd left 5 years before. I was an ordinary man. I'd been caught up in a war I didn't want. For five years I was a soldier. For five years I saw the horrors of war. It is something I've never forgotten.

I was lucky I lived to tell the tale.

Bill Ridgway interviewed Lawrence Oakes, known as Richard, who passed away after a short illness on Christmas Day, 1993. He shares a resting-place with his wife Bessie, who died two years earlier.

Richard's War

1. Sailed from Liverpool 1939
2. In South Africa (Ch3) 1939
3. Sailed to Bombay (now Mumbai) India (Ch4/5) 1940-1
4. Sailed to Basra in Iraq (Ch6) 1941
5. To Syria and Jordan (Ch7) 1941
6. To Egypt (Ch7) 1941
7. Tobruk, in Libya (Ch8/9) 1942
8. On hospital ship to Italy (Ch10) 1942
9. On the run in Italy (Ch11-16) 1943-4
10. Sent to Munich, Germany (Ch17) 1944-5
11. Flew back home (Ch18) 1945